REALLY TRULY

Autobiographies

Holly Prado

Green Tara Press
Los Angeles
2016

Green Tara Press
Los Angeles, CA
www.greentarapress.com

ISBN 978-1-945085-00-0 Paperback

Front cover art: "Moon Over East Hollywood (with cactus),"
watercolor and pen, by Holly Prado.

Back cover author photo: Alexis Rhone Fancher

Edited by Catherine Auman
www.catherineauman.com

Cover and interior design by
Lilly Penhall, Interstellar Graphics
www.interstellargraphics.com

DEDICATION

For Harry, always for Harry

WITH GRATITUDE TO
GREEN TARA PRESS

Green Tara Press is dedicated to publishing works that promote compassion, healing and love, and awaken and inspire readers to enlightened action.

Special thanks to Catherine Auman, editor/publisher of Green Tara, and to Lilly Penhall, book designer. Their efforts, both artistic and practical, have made this book possible.

TABLE OF CONTENTS

HOMESICK

1. SMALL CHILD

At age four, I loved the farm where Aunt Jeanette and Uncle Guy and their five children lived and worked. There were chickens in a little house all their own; a barn held cows for milking, plus two plough horses and two riding horses. Outside the barn, a huge sow inhabited a sty near a circular metal tank with water for the animals to drink from. Goldfish swam in the tank.

My mother, father and I often would drive the eighty-some miles from Lincoln, Nebraska, to a few miles outside of Sutton, Nebraska. Aunt Jeanette was Dad's sister; they'd always been close. My Cousin Jean, twelve years older than I was, let me in on whatever she was doing around the farm—riding, story-telling and singing, churning ice cream in a big wooden device, reaching under the hens on their nest to grab the egg or two underneath the warm chicken bodies.

I was surrounded by family, taken care of by everybody because I was the youngest. My parents had been married for ten years before I was born; they'd given up on having a child. In the 1940's, nobody deliberately waited that long to have children. I didn't understand I'd been unexpected. I was loved and cared for. And puzzled, frequently, about adult behavior, decisions made without my knowledge. So, one early September day, the weather still unrelentingly hot, I found myself on the farm with Aunt Jeanette and, it seemed, nobody else.

My mother and father had dropped me off for a few days so they could have a private vacation from me. They weren't going to travel. They were only planning some child-free leisure. They knew Jeanette was more than willing to have me around for awhile. The cousins had all gone back to school. Uncle Guy was busy with the hard work of farming. I followed Jeanette around, mostly in the kitchen where she always kept a round tin of home made chocolate chip cookies on top of the ice box—a real ice box for which a delivery man brought a massive chunk of ice every few days.

I slept upstairs in the two-story farmhouse. The long stairway between the first and second floors went up and up, then farther up. By the time I'd gotten to my room, I felt miles and years away from anybody.

The nights and the days were much too long. On the third day of my visit, I sought out Jeanette in the glider on the front porch, "taking a load off her feet," as she'd say. I climbed up next to her, leaned against her side. She put her arm around me and said, "You're homesick, aren't you?" I wasn't sure what "homesick" was exactly, but I got the word "home." I nodded. She and I rocked slowly in the glider. "Uncle Sam's coming. Maybe he'll take you back to Lincoln early."

Sam wasn't an uncle, really, but sort of. He was related to my father's mother's elderly sister; maybe he was her son. This wasn't clear in my mind. Sam was middled-aged, balding, unsmiling: I always felt he was worried about something. He'd been divorced. No one in our family ever got a divorce. He had a little boy my age named Chester Samuel. I liked that name, although it was long and hard to say. Where did Sam live? I was never sure. He stopped by at everybody's house from time to time for a meal and a visit.

So, Sam arrived. There was dinner at noon, a big meal with fried chicken (a couple of the henhouse hens), mashed potatoes, green beans cooked for a long time with bacon. Peach pie. Uncle Guy and his farmhands came in to eat and listen to the weather broadcast on the radio; farming relies on the weather, so nobody talked while the radio was on. After the pie, Jeanette packed my suitcase then got me into the front seat of Sam's car, next to him.

Sam was kind enough, telling me he'd have me home in a jiffy. His breath smelled like—what?—sweet gasoline? Not quite. As I grew up, I realized he'd been drinking liquor from a flask he had with him. I stayed as far from him as I could, my head against the car door, which was hard and hot.

I'd been lonely on the farm. I was lonely here with Sam. Sam must have been lonely himself as we moved along in silence, the great, flat prairie on either side of us stretching to the horizon. When we got to Lincoln, Sam took me home, but my parents weren't there. A neighbor said they'd gone to a picnic in the Missenbaugh's back yard. Sam knew where that was.

Maxine and Marlon Missenbaugh were long-time friends; so were the other adults gathered in the yard in their short-sleeved shirts and cotton print dresses. I let Sam help me out of the car; then, I ran, fast, across the lawn toward my mother and father. They saw me immediately, but instead of rushing to hug me, they stayed where they were, frowning. These were people who doted on me. How could they not be delighted to see me? Of course, I'd interrupted their privacy. Of course, this was a party for adults, something they'd had little time for in the years since I'd been born. Their childless lives of horseback riding, friendly parties and Masonic Lodge dances had pretty much disappeared. I would be a grown woman before I understood why they'd unceremoniously dropped me off at the farm: They wanted to be a youthful, free-wheeling couple again—if only for a few days. They believed I was old enough to have fun on my own with my aunt and the chickens, with the resident garter snake who lived under Jeanette's verdant green bean and pea vines next to the house. They'd forgotten that I was terrified of the snake.

Now, they recovered their poise and hurried to include me in the group photo that was being arranged. (My arrival with Sam had delayed the picture-taking.) I huddled in front of my mother. She held me close: Her body felt oddly unfamiliar, no longer Mother as Me, the same as Me, the one who completed Me. Her knees pressed into my back. I stood still, as I knew I needed to when somebody took a picture, but I wouldn't smile.

2. ILLNESS

"Your mother has a form of cancer," Dad told me. "Well," I thought, "if it's only a 'form,' then it's not really serious, not a big kind of cancer." I looked sideways at him as he drove: a handsome man with regular features, straight nose, solid cheekbones, firm chin with an appealing cleft in it. At age twelve, I found my parents to be the most attractive of any mothers and fathers I knew.

He kept driving, not pulling over or even slowing down to give me this news. We'd just bought the new, 1950 Chevrolet; he'd invited me to come along, try it out on the highway. But the real reason for the drive was to alert me to my mother's illness, which was truly serious, would become a big kind of cancer.

"Dr. Mueller is helping us," Dad said. "He's going to do surgery, and then we'll see." Roland Mueller, his wife and two daughters were friends. My parents trusted him; so, I did, too. Surely, I imagined, after whatever surgery he did, my mother would be fine.

She wasn't. She spent time in the hospital, off and on, until we moved from Lincoln, Nebraska, to Grand Rapids, Michigan, where she received good treatment but ultimately died four years after the diagnosis of stomach cancer. (Our re-location was suddenly necessary because Dad needed a job after the newspaper he worked for merged with the one other paper in Lincoln. The Grand Rapids Herald offered him a good Circulation Manager position. There was no other choice.)

Dad drove along steadily, asked if I had any questions. I shook my head. Even though I was a smart girl, I had no emotional vocabulary for suddenly feeling depleted, certainly not capable of being the adult I would need to be sooner than I'd imagined. Life was no longer as steady as the hum of the car under us.

* * * * * * * * * *

I liked sixth grade; Miss Hult encouraged me to write stories and plays. She was one of the "nice" teachers at Hartley Elementary School where I'd spent my entire school career to date. I got good grades; I took ballet and piano lessons; I had a best friend: Sondra Whalen, who wrote plays with me sometimes. We'd huddle in her bedroom on Saturdays where she'd throw a silky scarf over a lamp to cast an eerie glow. We wrote about witches until, once, the scarf started to smell like smoke. Sondra had to quickly get it off the lamp before her mother could rush in and find the room on fire.

We were graduating from Hartley Elementary School in two months, eager to get on to Northeast Junior High, which we envisioned as glamourous. Marilyn Miller, Bobbie Jorgensen, Sondra and I, along with Marilyn's mother, had a conference to discuss whether or not to wear lipstick on the first day of junior high. Would lipstick look cheap or make us appear as grown up as we wanted to seem?

As weeks went by, my mother remained a continuing, steady

presence for me. She didn't look any different; her reddish blond hair still curled, and she was still 5' 3" tall. She moved around the house with efficient grace. She understood how to listen to me without making judgments; how to paint my bedroom a new, soothing green; how to help me buy the bras I was starting to need. I could forget she was ill until I wanted a dress for the simple ceremony planned at Hartley for graduating sixth graders. My mother had been taken to the hospital for the second time. "I'll be your mother for now," Mrs. Whalen offered, generously. She was trying to fill in as kindly as possible. She helped me shop for an aqua-blue cotton dress with a little embroidery at the neckline. It was perfectly appropriate; I looked fine. But my mother had sewn the majority of my clothes from the time I was born. This dress wasn't my mother's design. It hadn't been stitched and hemmed and then ironed by my mother.

My mother would die. That's what nobody talked about in 1950; that's what was missing from my conversation with Dad in the car. My mother and I never mentioned her dying. She wanted to protect me from it. I'd wear light pink lipstick to junior high; I'd buy my first pair of one-inch "high heels"; other girls' mothers would help me find dresses until my mother died. Then, my father would re-marry, and my step-mother would try to steer my taste in clothes toward mature beiges, navy blues, grays.

The muteness I felt in the car, unconsciously realizing I'd be orphaned–the loss of one parent defines "orphan"–would take me beyond the simple inarticulateness of a twelve-year-old who'd never been challenged by life before. I'd go into myself, and then I'd go more deeply in. Part of me would never emerge. That part would become a creative source I've relied on for the individuality no one can have without tragedy. My mother–whom I still miss on a daily basis–gave me a great gift by dying: my introversion. My creative imagination.

I would inherit the gray Chevrolet when I was in high school and got a driver's license. I never adjusted to Michigan, but I studied hard while nurturing a secret desire to become a star in Broadway musicals. As I drove back and forth to school and on errands, I sang in the car. I sang with the windows rolled up. I sang only for the inner companion—that creative soul—which I trusted to take me where I needed to go.

3. EVENTUALLY JASMINE

My mother, alive for another year or so, sat next to my father in the front seat; I sat in back, looking past their heads to stare out at the lake. A "Great Lake" indeed, as large as the ocean, it seemed, since there was no land to be seen beyond it: Lake Michigan this first time I saw it—monotone gray water, the sand on the beach dull gray, gray sky echoing it all. Even in the car, I wore my heavy wool coat. It was March, 1953. The winter cold, the gray, would last until June.

We'd just moved to Grand Rapids. We'd driven to "see Lake Michigan! One of the Great Lakes!" Dad had said, thinking this would be a happy Sunday excursion. As we came up an incline and around a curve to find the lake extending below us, Dad said, trying a little too hard to be enthusiastic, "There it is!"

My hopes immediately diminished for anything good to come of our lives in this new place. My mother, usually willing to see the positive side of change, said nothing.

We sat parked by the side of the road for several minutes. No one was below us on the beach. The lake delivered small waves onto the shore then took them back again.

Silently, the three of us returned to our rented duplex in Grand Rapids. If Lake Michigan's vast expanse of sad water was the best our new home had to offer, I could only plan to get through high school and college as swiftly as possible, then move far away. I never caused trouble in school. I always did well; I liked to study. Making myself tame and compliant was a strategy I used to my advantage. And then, when I did run, I fled all the way to California, just as countless Midwesterners had done.

A month after I'd graduated from a small, insular college in the middle of Michigan, I'd gotten a clerical job in Los Angeles and a guest house to rent on Alvira Street in a neighborhood of 1930s and 40s Spanish Revival-style stucco homes, surrounded by plenty of palm trees and greenery. I took the bus downtown every day; when I came home in the evenings from work, I walked along Alvira Street, astonished. I'd found the Promising Unknown, the Something worth learning only for myself: bougainvillea, jacaranda, Tabebuia, Italian cypress, jimsonweed, eight varieties of geranium, jade plant, oleander, fig tree, eucalyptus, magnolia tree, night-blooming jasmine.

PEACE

I'd come to the top of a gradual slope, having kept my eyes on the marchers ahead of me to make sure I was walking with everybody else, when I sensed the crowd behind me and turned to look. My background is completely American; I was raised with ideals of equality (although my Midwestern family was firmly prejudiced, racially and religiously); Christian love (except for those who weren't Christian). The conflict between belief and actuality didn't escape me, even as a child, but I had no way to counter the hypocrisy until others did it for me. In the late 1950s and early 1960s, the Civil Rights Movement showed me what we could say and do as a country to stop injustice.

I looked back to see hundreds of people behind me, eight abreast in the street, all marching for peace, for an end to the VietNam war. Those waves upon waves of women and men that spring Saturday in 1967: This was the real force of democracy, the right of citizens to publicly protest national policy, fill the streets of San Francisco, stop traffic.

* * * * * * * * * * *

I'd gone to Albion College, a small liberal arts school founded by Methodists, where we all attended "chapel" twice a week to hear uplifting lectures designed to enhance our ethical standards. That was admirable, really, and I got a solid education, but I understood there was more. Something much, much more and much, much different from the poetry reading given in the chapel by Carl Sandburg. Yes, Carl Sandburg, aged and wispy and revered, the famous personification of early 20th century American poetry.

One midnight during my senior year, as I was falling asleep in my single bed in Susanna Wesley Hall, the women's dorm, I heard the growl of a man's voice coming from—it seemed—the wall right next to the bed. I got up, grabbed my robe. No men were allowed in the dorm. Had someone gotten past the watchful eye of the "house mother" after curfew? Or was there an emergency: a fire, or a bursting pipe in the bathroom down the hall?

As I headed into the hallway, I realized the voice was coming from the room next door to mine, where Char Crumb and Bobbie Bovee were roommates. I knocked. "Come in! But don't say anything!" they warned me. Inside the darkened room, I found the two young women in their pajamas, cross legged on the floor next to a lighted candle. They were listening to either a recording or a radio broadcast. "It's Allen Ginsberg reading 'Howl'," Bobbie hissed, motioning me to sit on the floor with them. I did. This man's voice and what he was saying was the "much, much more and much, much different" American poetry I was missing out on.

* * * * * * * * * * *

In 1960, twenty-two years old, I came to Los Angeles to make my way in the mysterious adult world. Ignorance attracts teachers:

By the time of the April 15, 1967, peace march, I'd made friends with Gary Hearty and his partner John McKinney; I thought I was in love with George Prado, a musician who'd become my husband. The gatherings at Gary and John's brought out an array of artists and creative spirits: One night, someone painted a voluptuous nude women surrounded by flowers on the living room carpet; he thought the beige of the rug too dull to bear. On Thanksgiving, a dozen people feasted, then simply shoved the table with its dinner plates laden with turkey scraps onto the patio, let our several dogs outside to enjoy the leftovers, closed the patio doors and went to sleep on the floor. We'd had our fill of martinis and marijuana and food.

I wasn't a hippie. I wasn't a political radical. I was an American who couldn't accept what I saw on television: VietNamese blown up by our troops; slaughter in villages; VietCong sympathizers blowing up our own soldiers. The terrible suffering, the convincing political intensity of my friends got me to San Francisco, to that peace march where I witnessed the power of joining together. John and Gary and George and I and our dogs—Polly the Boxer, Wigs the Mutt—had piled into Gary's VW Bug and headed north for this. "Dress middle-class," John told us. "Let the TV cameras know it's not just the radical fringe that wants peace."

I can't give myself credit for helping to create the social revolution of the 1960s. And, soon, I saw the whole movement collapse: Within the next four years, I'd be married and divorced; Gary and John would split up; drugs would ruin friends and strangers; there would be the homicidal fury of the Manson Family: Their victims included the La Biancas, whose home wasn't far from my own.

But for one moment in 1967, when I stared behind me at the force of peace to bring thousands of marchers together, I was convinced peace would come. Still marching, I shifted my view and saw, just across the street, a row of graceful Victorian houses.

There, on one second floor balcony stood Allen Ginsberg eating from a plate of spaghetti. His face was unmistakable; the black hair and beard were definitely his. Ginsberg's poetry had opened my mind to possibilities I'd never encountered in my college English Lit classes, in my reading of Charles Dickens, Thomas Hardy. When Ginsberg wrote "Howl," he wrote what I needed to know about my time. This was the present. This was California. This was *our* America. Ginsberg watched us, all of us. The legendary poet and Buddhist watched from his balcony. That was final proof that I was on the right path, up the rest of the slope and onward.

1973: SPRING

In a couple of months, I'd leave, forever, my job as an English teacher at Marshall High School. Divorced, without children, I lived alone, spending whatever spare time I had—never enough—writing. At age thirty-five, I was beginning to be published.

One Saturday night, 9:30 or 10:00 PM, I left my tiny upstairs apartment to take a walk, mail a letter. My Silverlake neighborhood was quiet, residential. I didn't hesitate to leave my door unlocked. The Los Angeles early spring air was cool; I wore jeans, a wool sweater, tennis shoes. In spite of the misery of the divorce, I felt less a failure than I had when I was married. I was throwing myself on the mercy of the universe, a force I blindly trusted to sustain me while I grappled with a writing life.

The letter got mailed. I was on my way home when a car slowed down next to me in the street. "Where's Sunset?" a guy shouted from the car window. "Turn right at the corner," I shouted back. "You'll run right into it." "Hey, come closer. I can't hear you." I didn't move closer. I kept walking.

I thought that was the end of it, but the car had quietly circled the block, driven back to me. One of the guys had gotten out. I didn't see or hear him. Then, he was behind me. He pulled one arm around my throat and shoved the other hand over my mouth, threatening me: "If you scream, I'll kill you." As soon as he moved his hand, I started screaming. He hit me, I guess. I felt nothing. I found myself on the ground, the attacker standing over me. I kicked at his balls as hard as I could, which at least kept him off balance. His partner got out of the car, stood nearby with a jagged broken bottle in his hand. But he looked scared; I didn't think he'd use the bottle. "Get the gun! Get the gun!" the first guy said, and the second man headed back toward the car. The two men were black; I'm white. Was this racial violence? Or was I simply an easy target, a woman alone? I didn't ask myself those questions. I just kept fighting.

After three minutes? Five minutes? a porch light went on across the street. Somebody had heard me scream. That was all it took to scare off the men—the knowledge that they'd been seen. The thugs jumped into their car, sped away, leaving me on the ground. I picked myself up, ran across the street to the small house with the porch light, where an older man said, "My wife has called the police."

The two cops wrote on their report, "Attempted kidnapping." That phrase frightened me more than the attack. "They wanted to get you in the car, rape you and kill you." The policemen were familiar with my description, vague as it was, of the men. "They're bad guys," one cop said. They drove me the few blocks home and told me they'd let me know if the men were arrested. Nobody smiled. Nobody wished me a pleasant evening.

I was okay. No broken bones or bleeding. No mental confusion. I did make sure to lock the door.

I woke up when someone, late the next morning, knocked.

When I opened the firmly locked door, my dad and stepmother stood smiling but were quickly horrified by my bruises. (They'd relocated from Michigan to Orange County, California, during my senior year in college; again, Dad had needed a new job.) This morning, they'd been to a church they liked in LA, thought they'd drop by, which they never did. Ever. I offered them coffee; they shook their heads. They were already worried because I was quitting a good job for a life of artistic instability. Depression-era hard workers, my dad's first response to my decision to leave high school teaching was, "But, honey, what will you do about your retirement?" Now, being attacked on a dark street at night by two potential murderers gave them even more reason to fear for me.

I ached all over. I had a black eye the size of a small planet. After I'd told Dad and Eleanor my story and reassured them, I rested all day on Sunday. I was grateful to be able to walk and talk. I'd survived a vicious encounter without permanent damage. On Monday, I went to school, told my teaching colleagues what had happened—the black eye was too obvious to ignore. I taught both Advanced Placement English and Remedial Reading. The AP students sympathized. The Remedial Reading kids did, too. I kept my description of the incident brief, but I told the truth. Why lie?

Remedial Reading students needed help because they'd failed to learn to read all the way through their school years. They weren't stupid or developmentally disabled. Usually, they couldn't concentrate. Or they'd had too many absences to keep up. Or their skills simply weren't the intellectual ones that would make them fluid readers and writers. I liked these teenagers. They had nothing to lose, so they didn't suck up to me. The AP kids had to get into college; they wanted "A's." They needed something from me, but the RR kids didn't. They were just glad I was nice to them.

At the end of my late morning RR class, after we'd written in journals, then read out loud (laboriously) a story and discussed what we'd read, as soon as the bell rang one boy—young man, really—who sat in the back made his way to me. He was wiry but muscular, restless, always moving around. He was Latino, with light skin, but he had the broad nose and full mouth of one African American parent. His curly, reddish hair was cut short. He'd never said much in class, never volunteered to answer questions. Now, he stood at my desk and said, "Miss? If you tell me where to find them, I'll beat up those guys for you." He was young enough and strong enough to do just that.

He waited while I thought about his offer. Finally, I said, "Thanks, Rudy. But the police are on it. I'm sure they'll catch the men." I didn't tell him I was one of those people who believes in peace and love and non-violence. I said thanks once more, told him I really appreciated his concern.

After that June, I wouldn't see Rudy or anybody from Marshall High again. Rudy's offer stays with me because he was the only one who was willing to take action to make things right for me. My parents were worried but had no real comfort to give. My friends and fellow teachers could only shake their heads, bemoan the fact that even the streets in a "good" neighborhood weren't safe at night. But Rudy would have risked himself in a fight if he knew that would even the score. His way wasn't my way, but who's to say how Divine Retribution is defined? I bow to the kid who could barely read but understood justice as he saw it and would act on his beliefs in defense of someone victimized. I think the Powers that Be would honor that, too.

CHAGALL

The friends I was traveling with had scattered to other parts of the museum. I had the room to myself as I stood in front of a woman sleeping, floating, her arm flung above her head, sustained by an oval, womb-like background of deepest reddish-pink. A donkey merges with this background, and to the right, outside the cocoon, stands an angel-protector. I burst into tears. The woman's restfulness, her luscious sensuality, the tenderness with which she, the animal, the angel have been painted—art as sacred love.

I was shocked at the force of my tears once they'd begun. They didn't stop while I was absorbed in Chagall's "Song of Songs" series on the walls. All the donkeys, lovers, winged creatures, large avian presences—I stared and wept. In one painting, a hand, fingers gently curved, reaches toward a crescent moon with the most delicate desire imaginable. In another, the heads of two lovers become part of the whole world, not dominating it, but inhabiting it as part of a fabulous whole that includes a fat, multi-colored sun nourishing it all.

I'd been away from home for weeks; I wasn't even sure what "home" meant to me now, but here I was in Nice, France, at The Musee National Message Biblique Marc Chagall. This was August, 1976. I'd become a writer in the past six years; I'd see two books of mine published when I got back to Los Angeles. This surprised me. I'd had no expectations involving writing, especially poetry.

Everything surprised me about this time in my life: My musician husband suddenly left me in 1971. I wasn't the one who'd wanted to get married in the first place. I was teaching high school English, thought this would be my career. But I'd started to write. Then, I was asked to give a few readings. Poems were published; manuscripts accepted. I quit my teaching job. What the hell? I had no husband, no children, nobody to take care of but me. I moved into a tiny apartment with a view of quiet hills. I set up my typewriter so I could see those hills and simply think, think as much as I needed to, then write everything down just to see what those thoughts would look like on the page.

I'd quit my teaching job in 1973. I worked one year for Poets in the Schools because of a grant from the Department of Labor to "make poets employable." During 1973-74 because of that job, poets who are still my friends and creative companions came into my life. Then, after a year of substitute teaching, I was convinced to resign from the public school system forever. In 1975, I helped organize a national women writers' conference at the Woman's Building in Los Angeles. I made writer-friends, opened myself to possibilities for a feminine approach to writing—autobiographical, imagistic, passionate—that I knew wasn't only feminine, but it was compelling to understand it that way. I'd come from a family in which women were educated, respected, so to see what seemed like the entire country become aware of women's rights, women's potential, women's creative intensity—that was thrilling. Pretty quickly, I figured out ways to teach creative writing, to earn enough to live on. Early in the summer of 1976, I taught a two week, intensive writing workshop which paid $1,500.00, exactly the amount I needed to take a trip to England and France.

So, I found myself in August traveling with my gay friends Gary, Jim and Fred, who all spoke French, were willing to do the driving and organizing, could guide me. Here in the Chagall Museum, I let go of my earnestness, of my need to overcome the sad divorce, the impact of changing my life completely in order to write. I cried because for all my certainty that I'd made the right changes for myself, I hadn't considered love that reflected Chagall's fullness of spirit, sweetness of soul.

In these paintings, I could see what was missing: There wasn't a loving home inside of me, within my own heart. Here, I could see the possibilities for having both art and love. As I stood weeping, I noticed a museum guard, a man only a little older than I was, looking at me. He watched me cry. When he caught my eye, he smiled a one-side-of-the-mouth French smile that usually meant disdain; this smile, though, was understanding. I felt caught in what I'd thought was a purely private moment, but I felt less lonely, too. He'd evidently seen what I'd seen in Chagall's work.

I moved on to the chapel within the museum where Chagall's stained glass windows illuminated the space. I sat down; I'd stopped crying. Such blues in those windows, blues worthy of heaven. Chagall had found this heaven; he'd let me have some of it for an afternoon. For longer, really, a lot longer. It's been thirty-seven years since that trip. But I still see my younger self in front of the "Song of Songs," realizing how much beauty, how much love we can embrace through paint, through language, through the holiness of imagination, if we can just bring ourselves to bear it.

TRAVEL

I received a miracle at El Santuario de Chimayo, the small church in Northern New Mexico where healings occur. Crutches, trusses and walking sticks arrayed on the walls testified to the power of the place, a nothing-much church in terms of religious glitz, but a widely recognized Holy Source. The exterior of the sanctuary was cave-shaped, a natural adobe-tan. Deep inside the church, a round hole full of curative soil exposed to view was potent enough to make me feel faint, and I never feel faint.

A driving trip to the Southwest in 1977: My friend Jane Ellison had planned the route; she did the driving. Her mother Ann and I watched the scenery go by as we moved from Los Angeles to Arizona to New Mexico. Santa Fe and Taos, of course, attract artists of all kinds. I understood, though, as soon as we entered the land of mesas, silversmiths and turquoise-painted doorways that this place didn't want me. Generations of dead Native Americans haunted the landscape. I heard their whispers. I sensed disapproval everywhere—of me, of tourists, of artists, of all those encroaching. I wanted to go home, to go back to Harry, the man I'd just fallen in love with who would be the love of my life.

The church at Chimayo felt as alien as every other site we'd visited. At the back, the small room of healing power was packed with locals and tourists, all straining to get a look at the mysterious hole in the floor. I'm not Catholic; my religious life exists in a nexus of ancient traditions and idiosyncratic personal experiences. I expected nothing to come of my quick prayer in front of the ugly pit full of damp dirt. But my need was recognized by—what?—who ever knows? I had sensed the force of the room, the believers, the strange dirt; I was woozy. But was that a supernatural presence or simply the heat and pressure of all the bodies crowded around the hole?

The next morning before we even left our hotel, my prayer was miraculously answered. I hadn't prayed for anything Religiously Marvelous, yet my request was urgent at that moment in my life. I believe in revealing everything in writing, but the specifics will have to remain a secret. Divine intervention deserves reverence— and silence. When the supernatural has so obviously heard a prayer, so directly responded, there's nothing to do but shut up. "Mystery" as a word has its roots in "a closed mouth."

What I can say is that even when the circumstances, the territory, the history of a locale are wrong and foreign and dismissive, there can be a sudden embrace: love at its most obscure—yet vividly present. I had no right to be where I was, but in the moment I said a prayer for help, I was forgiven.

INDIANS

"Yep, we had a relative who was scalped by the Indians and lived to tell about it," my father said from time to time when I was a child. That was all he said; it was all he knew.

We were in Nebraska, a Plains state where the Arapaho, Kiowa and Cheyenne had made their homes long before we—or any Anglo-Europeans—arrived; The Great Sioux Nation hunted in Nebraska without making any permanent settlements. I loved the Indians.

Well, I loved the idea of Indians: the teepees and horses, the beautiful clothes made from softened deer and elk hides, the eerie chants. I loved buffalo, of course, since the Sioux were a buffalo culture, relying on the huge creatures for meat, skins, ritual. On the outskirts of Lincoln, Nebraska, my own home, was Pioneer Park, with its small herd of American Bison which we visited some Sundays. (By the 1940s, a nearly extinct buffalo population was gradually being restored.) I stood at the fence separating me and the animals, staring at the gorgeous, pre-historic-looking, sternly mute buffalo, much more enchanted by them than by the adorable kitties and puppies most little girls loved.

Until I was ten or eleven, I was sure I could grow up to be a Sioux chief. That was my career of choice, especially because I'd get to wear an enormous feather headdress. I didn't know that each feather of each headdress was earned by the performance of a brave act. Before a feather was presented to a man, he purified himself with fasting and meditation. The headdresses were sacred, not simply fun to strut around in. I didn't know anything, really, about these peoples. My relationship to everything about the Indians was fantasy and the desire for exotic beauty. It was my own inner Indian I loved; it was the Otherness of our country that was missing from my small, protected, bookish, WASP girlhood. Roaming the Plains on horseback; living in a tent that was painted with events and symbols; wearing a buffalo robe—yes, I was sure that was the life for me. But that life no longer existed. During my childhood, all that glamour was in my imagination; the Plains Indians were restricted to reservations scattered here and there.

During my Campfire Girl days at Hartley Elementary School, our leader Mrs. Petersen contacted an Indian reservation to arrange for our troupe to visit, to learn about the way Indians lived in the present. Every Campfire Girl had a fake Indian name; we were awarded colored wooden beads for completing tasks—crafts, science experiments, animal care and so on. But when I was invited to go on the trip, I was terrified. Real Indians! Not my imaginary tribe but actual people who might—do what? Scalp me?

* * * * * * * * * * *

Many years later, I was with my cousins Jennifer and Abby Anstey in a rented car driving toward Yellowstone Park where we were joining others from my father's side of the family for a reunion. "Was there somebody in our family who was scalped by Indians and lived to tell about it?" I asked, looking out at the Tetons, eager to see Yellowstone with its geysers and mud pots and elk and—yes—buffalo.

"Scalp Woman!" both of them exclaimed. "No. *She* scalped the Indians." They told me the story: Hannah Dustin, in March of 1697, had a farm with her husband and family (twelve children!) near Haverhill, Massachusetts. Abinake Indians in war dress attacked the farm, capturing Hannah while the rest of the family got away safely. Her one-week-old baby was wrenched from her arms and murdered. Hannah was forceably marched through the countryside for several days. At a temporary encampment, she met a boy who'd been held captive for a year or so. Together, they plotted an escape, and on March 31st the two of them managed to kill ten Indians, scalp them and make it down the Merrimack River to Hudson, New Hampshire. Today, near Concord, NH, there's a plaque dedicated to Hannah along with an imposing statue. The plaque refers to her as a "famous symbol of frontier heroism." Supposedly, the governor of New Hampshire awarded Hannah Dustin a silver cup for her bravery, but, as Jean, Abbey and Jennifer's mother has said wryly, "Nobody in the family's ever seen that cup."

Stories about white women being kidnapped by Indians are sometimes true and sometimes only rumor, fear of "savages" fueling fictional accounts of the horrors experienced by wives and daughters in the hands of brutes. Hannah's story is well documented, although killing as many as ten Indians seems an exaggeration. Certainly, Cynthia Ann Parker, the young woman whose history serves as the basis for the film "The Searchers," was factual; while in captivity she became the mother of Quanah Parker, later a prominent Comanche figure.

During the social reconfigurations of the 1960s, "Indians"

became Native Americans, a much more accurate term than "Indian," which refers to the false impression by early European explorers that they'd landed in India, not North America. Because of my personal love of a private Other, I still think "Indian" when I remember the fascination I had with my own version of history when I lived on the land of the Sioux, Arapaho, Cheyenne, Kiowa.

* * * * * * * * * *

In my mid-thirties, I needed to turn deeply inward. The psychology of C.G. Jung was intriguing; I started a long path of analytical work. Dreams were important. I wrote down everything I recalled, and I struggled to untangle the images sent by the unconscious, knowing those images could illuminate a whole side of my psyche that had been hidden. Working with the opposites in oneself is at the basis of a lot of Jungian ideology, and, sure enough, I had dreams of Native Americans that reminded me of how meaningful my childhood fascination had been to me. I believed I could *be* an Indian. I believed there were mysteries and mythologies available to me if only I had the resources to connect with them. My dreams became those resources: I began to understand how a relationship with one's opposite selves, with The Other, could bring personal fulfillment, and could foster outer peace with people whose race, ethnicity, religion, language, viewpoint were vastly different from my own.

Three "Indian" dreams:

Early on in my analytical work, I dreamed of a virile, muscular Native American man who captured me and held me to the ground. As he loomed over me, I was sure he'd rape me. Instead, he lectured me on a way to tell time that relied on more natural methods than clock-time. He was urgent in his need to impress on me the

33

idea that I didn't have to tell time as rigidly as I thought.

Some years later, I dreamed I was in a cave-like, communal gathering place with a few others. An elderly Native American figure, a man who commanded great respect, imparted a particular wisdom I was ignorant of: There is a language for each sign of the zodiac, he said. He would teach each person present her/his special language, based on astrology. He singled me out to tell me he'd teach me to "speak Taurus," since I was born under the sign of the bull. Within my inner Indian life was a language pertaining to the heavens, the zodiac of the skies, but also to me personally. The Indian self and the white self cooperated in creating a complete identity, sharing a language that reflects the power of both the universal and the personal self.

The third dream occurred only a few weeks ago: I'm walking down a wooden stairway, rubbing my shoe against little holes in the stairs where spit has collected, cleaning off the spit, sending it under the stairs to the ground. To my surprise, near the bottom of the stairway is a cluster of six or seven Native American men, very much Plains Indians with their long, black braids and their red breech cloths. They're busily cleaning the stairs of spit, too, using soap and water. They don't look up as I pass them. I say, "Thank you, thank you," but they don't acknowledge me. They come to me not for praise or recognition but to share the work within the psyche—as they always have, whether I've understood that or not.

When Jennifer, Abby and I got to Yellowstone, we were handed a bright yellow leaflet at the entrance, warning us not to try to pet the buffalo. "They can outrun you and do damage," the warning said. We were told that the animals in Yellowstone take precedence over the people, so one morning when I came across a buffalo lounging on the grass in front of the restaurant where I was headed, I gave it plenty of room to do exactly what it was doing: Letting me know that it and its kind had been on this earth since pre-history, unlike my puny, contemporary, human self.

Right now on my desk is a postcard: a 1908 Edward Curtis photograph of "The Eagle Catcher," believed to be Sioux, probably from northwestern Nebraska. The man stands on a rocky precipice overlooking broad prairie. He's wearing an eagle—wearing an entire eagle, which extends from his shoulders to his hips and encloses him in its feathered body. This is what I needed as a child; what I still need: the Indian's breadth of experience with the natural world, his belonging to that world—no, his *being* that world, reaching out to take on the possibility of flight. In my most fundamental American imagination, this is my possibility, too: joining the original spirit I always called "Indian," to go beyond the known, to earn the feathers for that headdress I once thought could be mine.

TRAIL

I hiked there often in the 1970s and 80s. On a weekday morning, early, I'd see no one, or perhaps, occasionally, a person alone or a couple walking a dog. Once, I did follow a man and a woman and their Golden Retriever up and up, not paying much attention to them, just thinking, which I could do as much as I needed to on that trail. Then, suddenly I realized that two coyotes had joined the dog, who was a little distance behind the couple. The coyotes smelled around, loped beside the dog for a bit then retreated—wild, long-bodied, sly—down a slope into the underbrush. Something brutal could have happened; it didn't.

On this trail through the hills in Griffith Park over the course of several years, I did come across two diamond back rattlesnakes, one alive and one dead. Also, a grand deer emerged one morning, a buck with imposing antlers and steady gaze. He stood with the intense stillness of all deer. He stared from his place a few yards off the trail as I carefully kept my even stride, not hurrying but not stopping, either. Nature deserves its rightful place, and I, even in the middle of Los Angeles, was the stranger here. I loved the odor in the air during late summer and early fall, before the rains: dusty, weedy, herbal. Southern California, away from its imported overlay of prettiness, is wild tobacco and jimsonweed.

What was I thinking about as I hiked? Myself, I suppose, in those years when I began to untangle the young woman I'd been so she would be free to leave the older self I was becoming. There were no more youthful choices to be made. I loved a man and his child. I loved my work. I loved my willingness to persist, to not give up on learning how to live with my flaws and the flaws of the world. Nature is indifferent; it helped me to be somewhere that treated me neutrally, disinterestedly.

The Griffith Park trail, across from the Greek Theater, was one I hiked often. The rattlesnakes were rare shocks, but they belonged to the park; all I had to do was respect them, whether they were curving sinuously along the hillside or lying, inert, in the middle of the trail. So, on the morning I came across love, I'd been to the top of the trail, to the paved road that signaled civilization, where I'd turned around and was heading down for another half an hour, back to my car and home.

The slight chill in the air was autumnal; the shrubs and weeds along the way were stalky, brittle. Suddenly, I rounded a blind curve to find two men with their pants down around their ankles, having sex in the middle of the trail. There wasn't time to turn away. Of course, now aware of me, they scrambled into their clothes as they laughed nervously, embarrassed. Their bodies were slender, pale-skinned, smooth. I was frightened for them, because I knew the police patrolled this part of the park and arrested gay men for having sex here. I thought of telling the two men this, but they probably already knew. I was an intruder whose most graceful course of action was to simply move on, eyes on the trail.

I couldn't forget what I saw, which made me consider—over a long time—how I believe love should be. Some people enjoy risky sex; others choose celibacy. Eros has his own ideas about each of us. In my own erotic imagination I came to this: Whether it's casual sex or a thirtieth wedding anniversary, lovemaking deserves a wide bed with clean, light blue sheets; late afternoon light filters through breeze-stirred curtains. A little music? Maybe. The important thing is privacy, a secret we keep because each of us knows she or he is the only human being ever to have these feelings, these desires and their fulfillment. The rasp of sharp-stemmed bushes against our skin, the glimpse of a coyote pack watching from a little distance, a sudden figure who appears around the curve to ruin everything—no.

Someone I know is dying too gradually, too young. Someone dear to me has had a daughter kidnapped by her mother, who has disappeared. Then, the news that Connie Aldrich—an ample, gregarious girl of seventeen when we graduated from high school together—is gone. Her memorial service will be this weekend. Personal tragedy tells everybody's story, so in the truth of that don't we deserve a little honey on the tongue, tasty kissing and hugging and finally lying back on those sheets feeling confident in our willing bodies once again? Nature's indifference is cleansing and cruel, but human beings need all their merciful warm-bloodedness.

I'd like to know what became of those two young men, now much older. I want to be reassured. Of course, they're lost to me except in memory. I turn to what's at hand for proof that love is ultimately sustenance, comfort. Here's what I see, turning the blind curve at the end of this particular day: My husband is writing down, step by step, my recipe for linguine with garlic oil, anchovies, pine nuts and parmesan cheese. He wants to learn this favorite dish so that, as he says, "If you ever get sick and can't cook, I can make it for you."

BYSTANDER

The time of night to think about going to bed: I was relaxing at my desk in the study, which faces Mariposa Avenue. Suddenly, I heard, "I'm not a prostitute! I'm not a whore!" coming from across the street. I opened the curtain. There was a police car. There was a cop running along the street; he chased a heavy-set woman, the one who was shouting.

I went outside to see how this got resolved. It was July 1, 1996, when there were hookers on Sunset Boulevard, a long block north of our house. Sometimes, they solicited men in cars, ended up on our quiet, residential street. The police had spotted the woman either approaching a client or getting out of a car. They were arresting her, or trying. She ran fast. All I could see in the dark from my side of the street was that she was light-skinned, had straw-like, bleached blond hair and wore a frothy white summer dress. The dress wasn't especially sexy. It looked like a high school party dress. Was she a prostitute? I didn't know. She said she wasn't. The police believed otherwise.

The cop caught the woman by the arm. With the help of his partner, she was put into the back seat of the police car. "Okay," I thought, "That's the end of that." I went back into the house. In the study again for only a few minutes, I heard more commotion outside—a car starting up then screeching to a halt; more running sounds; a shot.

Of course, I dashed out, along with neighbors who'd heard the shot, too. The first policeman, the one who'd chased the woman originally, was leaning over her as she lay on the sidewalk. He was saying, "Stay with us. Please just stay with us." Pleading with her to live.

More police cars arrived. An ambulance. My neighbors and I shook our heads at each other, sad about the gunshot and the woman and the cop who was young, hadn't started his evening on the job, I was sure, wanting to shoot anybody.

Again inside my house, I began to get ready for bed. But someone knocked at the door: a handsome cop, the soft-spoken guy in the well-pressed uniform they send to politely ask you "a few questions." I hadn't seen the actual shooting; I wasn't really a witness. He still wanted me to come to the Hollywood Division police station, talk to a detective. I saw that although it was midnight, and I was teaching a class the next morning, I was going to have to let the seemingly kindly officer escort me to a police car. He'd wait while I got my purse and a sweater—even July evenings in LA get chilly.

The sound-proofing tile was coming loose from the wall of the detective's tiny office. Dull green paint on the walls was peeling. My first thought was that the city of Los Angeles wasn't taking good care of its police force. There was barely space in the room for a desk and chair, along with the chair where I sat. The detective: middle-aged, serious but not gruff. "Is the woman dead?" I wanted to know, before he could ask me anything.

He nodded yes, then explained what had happened: Somehow, the woman had managed to move from the back of the police car to the front seat. The keys were in the ignition. She started the engine, nearly ran over the arresting policeman's partner, who was standing in front of the car. She came to a sudden halt, got out, began to run again. The cop who'd caught her to begin with shot at her. The shot killed her.

I told the detective what I'd seen. I wasn't worth questioning beyond this one interview. Three of my neighbors, young Filipinos, had been brought to the police station, too. They'd been outside watching the action for longer than I had. Two of the kids, about ten and twelve years old, were children of the family across the street from our house. The third was a visiting cousin about their age. He lived on Guam. "It's a little island," he whispered, as we all, finally, got into a car that would take us home. "Nothing like this ever happens there."

Poor kid. Poor woman. Poor cop who killed someone "in the line of duty." Poor all of us. On the way home, the cheerful—even at 2 AM—plain clothes officer at the wheel, said to me, "Hey, this will make good conversation around the water cooler tomorrow." He hadn't been at the scene; he had no idea what really went on.

"It was a tragedy for everybody," I told him, angry—suddenly furious—that he'd tried to make light of the shooting.

The next morning, a TV reporter, a woman I recognized from local newscasts, showed up at our door. "I told the police what I know," I said. I declined to be interviewed on camera. As she got back into the big TV van parked at our curb, I thought, "How dare you? You've never been the least bit interested in our neighborhood until now, until somebody's dead in the street."

For days afterward I felt the woman's presence, an eerie disturbance in the air outside where she'd been killed: her spirit unsettled, lost. In the study where I'd heard the shot, I could feel the woman searching, too. She needed help. On the good advice of a friend, I bought a sage bundle, lit it and smudged our house, cleansing it psychically, telling the woman it was all right to "go home" now, wherever her soul-home might be.

That worked. And I added her to my list of the dead which I read out loud on Dia de los Muertos, November 2nd, every year, asking for blessings. I don't know her name, so I can only describe her. I see her in that white, frilly party dress. It's always night, but her dress stands out against the darkness.

SCAM

"Honey! Hey, honey!" A young woman leans out of her car window to shout at me. She's on the passenger side; the driver has pulled up next to me as she goes on, "You hit my car! Pull over!" she insists. So, I do pull over to a shady spot along Fountain Avenue, heading toward Trader Joe's to buy cheese and wine. I don't remember even getting close to her car. I've never seen her car—or her—before.

As soon as her car parks behind me, she jumps out, talking fast. "You just barely scraped me," she says. "You can see the marks on both our cars." I walk around the cars. Yes, I can see minor scratches on the fenders of her car and mine. As I stand next to my car, I see two men in hers: The driver is tall, muscular, scowling. The guy in the back seat leers out the window, grinning. His buck teeth are horribly crooked and stained. They look as if they've been sharpened. He spits out, "We're from Sacramento."

She explains, "We're visiting our grandmother in the hospital here." Then, confidently, "I'll call my uncle; he's got a repair shop at home. What's your name, honey?"

"Holly. What's yours?"

"Jane. I'll just take a picture of the damage on my car, send it on my phone to my uncle, get an estimate for repairs." Around our little group, the world quiets. There's no traffic noise, although cars whoosh past. Nobody approaches on the sidewalk or comes out of a shop to see what's going on.

I don't look at the photo. I don't ask to talk to the uncle. I don't argue with her when she speaks into the phone, saying, "Are you sure? $575.00? Is that the best you can do?" Pause. "Okay. I understand. Thanks."

She has abundant reddish-brown hair, a sweater to match it. The sweater is off-the-shoulder, has sparkly decorations across the chest. "I'm sorry, honey. The repairs to my car will be $575.00."

I don't tell her and her brothers, as she refers to them, to follow me to my mechanic a couple of miles away to get an estimate from him. I don't tell her she's full of shit, although I think she and her brothers deliberately scraped my fender in the Von's supermarket parking lot then followed me when I left. Whatever the truth is, I'm silent. I do as she asks, which, of course, results in my going home, followed by Jane and the brothers. They park in front of my house, watch as I go in, get cash, return and hand it to Jane. The men haven't left the car; Jane stands beside it. I ask her to sign a receipt and give me her phone number and license plate number. She scribbles it all on the piece of paper I hand her. When I check, I see that she's written one wrong license plate number, which I'll correct–pointlessly–when I go back into my house.

I cross the street toward home. When I turn to look, I see Jane counting the cash, holding it close to her eyes, making sure every bill is in place. As soon as she hops back into the car, they take off–fast. I've never seen them again.

Once in awhile, it's necessary to give the devil his due. Jane and her brothers are small demons, nothing as fierce as real evil, which takes possession of serial killers, torturers, child murderers. I got off cheap. And, I believe, I may have averted something worse, much worse in my vulnerable life. Really, what convinced me to be silent, to play along, to give these people what they wanted was the guy in the back seat. Those teeth.

STREET

August 20, 2009: At 7:30 AM, I'm standing in my pajamas in the middle of our street, Mariposa Avenue, East Hollywood, Los Angeles, California, holding out my hand to the person lying face down on the pavement, "Do you want me to help you up?" I ask.

"I asked him to help me up," he mutters, gesturing toward a tall, African American man with a shopping cart full of recyclable bottles and cans, who's hesitating on the sidewalk, waiting to see what happens. "He doesn't have to help you up," I say. I've been listening from inside our apartment to the loud, whiny pleas of this man—is he a man?—after he toppled from the curb where he was sitting.

He reaches toward me, takes my hand and pulls himself to his feet. He's thin. His tight-fitting, pink pants are dirty, dirtier than they'd be from the not-very-serious fall he's taken. We're facing each other as he rights himself. "Are you okay?" I ask.

"I'm just too drunk to walk."

"Do you have a place to stay?"

He waves one arm in a general westerly direction, toward Sunset Boulevard, or maybe the freeway underpass where people sometimes live. "I have a tent over there." Pause. Then, "I'm sort of homeless."

In the thirty years I've lived on Mariposa Avenue, I've had—and still have—neighbors who are Peruvian, African-American, Filipino, gay, Mexican, Armenian. I say "goodmorninghowar-eyou" to hookers, gang guys, white Anglos like me; to young film makers, actors, musicians, visual artists. I nod to grandfathers pushing babies in strollers and to Armenian vegetable truck drivers whose vans carry not only cucumbers and eggplant but silky print dresses to sell. I never miss a chance to find meaning in these people and encounters. What do they say for our neighborhood's mythology—the mythology of multiplicity, difference, conflict or co-existence? What invisible powers might be at work to bring us together for its own purposes?

Half an hour earlier: Still in bed, I'd heard the homeless man outside our window where he sat on the front stairs, near the street. He'd shouted, "You're a fucking asshole!" to nobody I could hear answer back. I got up, went outside to grab the *LA Times* from the front patio. When I saw his disheveled hair—yellow, not blond but yellow like a Crayola—and the glumly stoned or drunk or generally confused profile, I said sternly, "Could you please move on? My husband's asleep."

He got up immediately, teetered down the street in a fake-fem-inine, hip-swaying, wobbly way. When he saw the man collecting bottles and cans from trash bins lining the street, he tried to make friends. The man was having none of it. Back in the house, I was sorry I'd been curt. I was reminded of someone I'd written about a couple of years ago, someone sexually uncertain, who appeared to want to cross a boundary toward identity. I recalled boundaries of

47

my own I'd had to negotiate. So, to make up for my harshness, at 7:30 I headed outside again as soon as I heard the pleas for help to stand up. I took a twenty dollar bill with me.

Now, after he's on his feet, I'm standing with him in the middle of the street, face to face. He suddenly declares, "I love you!" opening his arms, enveloping me in an effusive hug.

"No, you don't." How can he possibly love me? We're complete strangers.

"I do! I love unconditionally. I love everyone unconditionally."

I consider this as I pull away. I like wild spiritual ideas. This one isn't new, but it's unexpected from somebody whose T-shirt is full of primary-color squiggles and a message I can't decipher. The T-shirt is as stained and unsavory as his pants.

"That's great," I tell him, "but it can get you into trouble." A vulnerable drunk staggering around this neighborhood hugging everybody sounds to me like a recipe for assault—or worse.

"I've fucked up. I want to go to AA," he says.

"You can get un-fucked up. You'll get a lot of support at AA meetings."

My eyes are level with his chest; I notice two small, soft breasts under the T-shirt. I ask, "Are you transsexual?" No hesitation. "Yes."

"There's a large transsexual community in Hollywood."

"There is?"

I can't believe he doesn't know this. Why would he be drawn to this part of Los Angeles if he didn't think he'd find people here like himself? Herself? "Ask around," I tell him. "You could get help from that community, too."

I hand him the twenty dollar bill. "Get some breakfast. Get sober. You're young; you have gifts you haven't even discovered yet." He steps back, presses his hands against his chest. "You totally read me!" he exclaims. "I'm twenty-four years old." I haven't thought about his actual age, but twenty-four! That's really, really young. He has a lifetime ahead of him. I can't "read" him; I have no particular insight into this stranger.

He steps forward, hugs me again. I don't object. He seems truly moved by our exchange, yet I also understand that drunks are notorious liars. "I love you!" he insists.

Do I believe this or not? He stands in the middle of a street, homeless, at the mercy of the city and his own bad habits. Yet, he has a religious impulse toward unconditional love. When I think about what this might mean, I remember Hermes, the mercurial Greek god of sudden chance with his blessings and his tricks. Hermes holds both male and female within himself and has been described as "undignified but never vulgar." In spite of unexpected appearances and disappearances, he's known as the friendliest of the gods, which pretty much sums up the person hugging me. After a minute or two, I release myself. "Get some breakfast, okay?"

The African American has disappeared; he retreated, gladly I'm sure, when he saw the drunk was occupied with me. I turn to go home.

"God bless you!" he shouts, this transsexual in pink pants, badly-cropped hair dyed glaring yellow, dark stubble on his chin, little breasts vulnerable.

"I do take that as a blessing," I shout back. "God bless you, too." Whatever god he believes in, I hope that Hermes in his role as a guide between worlds is helping him keep his precarious balance as he makes his way into the rest of the uncertain morning.

WOMAN

I.

I say hello to her as we get in or out of the swimming pool at the Y on the mornings we both show up for aquafitness classes. She's come to recognize me as a regular, so offers me a brief smile.

My Nebraska farm aunts had broad, uncharismatic Anglo-Saxon faces on which they wore no make-up. They carried the early pioneers' emotional reticence, the need to persevere no matter what came to them.

The woman at the Y has the same solid, bold-cheek-boned features as my aunts, the same self-restraint.

Because those aunts shaped me when I was a child, and because I never truly knew who they were, I watch the woman at the Y carefully.

2.

Like the rest of us, she came to the pool to stay in shape. Older, bulky—not fat but doughy—at first, she yanked her hair back in a messy little pony tail. One morning, she hissed at a woman who was crowding her, saying, as a threat, "I have words." This made me believe she'd been an English teacher who relied on words to control restless classes. I'd been an English teacher for a few years myself.

That ratty little chunk of hair behind her head, wrapped too tightly—painfully—in a rubber band, told me she fought with her body. Now, she was retired, I believed, free from schools and strict routines. Now, though, she might ...

3.

A story without climactic action is life: the gradual unfolding of days: We eat. We bathe—with our favorite lavender soap or with whatever's on sale at the supermarket. We watch movies, read Jane Austen or Don DeLillo, gossip with the two or three friends we love and trust. We curse misfortune. We exercise our curiosity:

I have little interest in plot, but I love sequence. This then this then this until everything that makes us human has been included. The anguish of my aunts' stoic self-containment was that I couldn't hear about their sorrow or their lust or their religious fervor or their loneliness. They were always and forever "The Aunts." They taught me to pick peas, to kill chickens, to start a fire in a wood stove. They taught me the practical world, as if it were the only world.

4.

The winter I was four years old, my mother, father and I lived in an apartment building in downtown Lincoln, Nebraska, while our house was being remodeled. One afternoon, I wandered into the hallway on the third floor, then into the elevator. I rode down, then up. When the elevator suddenly stopped and the doors slid apart, I got out. At the end of the hallway was an apartment with its door open. I heard the sound of a vacuum cleaner. Thinking my mother was vacuuming, I walked into the apartment, exactly like ours—but not really, not at all. The woman I saw, concentrated on her chore as I paused on the threshold, was a stranger.

I had no grandmothers: one had died before I was born; the other was uneducated, inarticulate and completely uninterested in me. My mother, although kind, would die of cancer—too young—without including me in her illness, her thoughts about dying, her hopes for me. I still wonder what she believed would make me happy. In a move from Nebraska to Michigan, the aunts were left behind. After my mother died, my father quickly remarried. At age sixteen, an only child, I realized I had to puzzle out a life for myself. Everyone became a stranger, like the "mother" in the wrong apartment.

5.

Within a year after she'd joined the Y, the woman I like to watch had followed a sensible diet, lost twenty pounds. She'd gotten a chin-length, stylish haircut. Her gray hair hung softly near her face. Her swimming suits—she's in the pool three or four times a week—fit her well; one features tangerine-orange, yellow, lime jungle flowers.

She hasn't been especially forthcoming, but now in the pool she wears her lively suits and keeps little gold earrings in her ears as she jogs, does jumping jacks, extends her arms and legs in cross country skiing motions.

6.

This past Wednesday morning, 9:00 AM in the pool, as Karen (our instructor) puts exercise music on the Y's unreliable CD player, the woman hears the music, shouts, "I love Zumba!" Karen's uncertain—is this Afro-Latin-Belly-Dancing rhythm too fast, too raucous for a class of arthritic old ladies?

When Karen asks if the music is too much for us, I call out, "It's fine." This immediately puts me on the woman's side, so she—swaying and twisting—tells me she knows I'm a teacher, then pours out the details of her high school teaching career and her belief that "standardized tests are ruining education." She did teach English; I was right about that but not about the person who's been unleashed by Zumba rhythms. She laughs—it's a throaty, 2 packs of cigarettes a day laugh. Karen turns up the music a little more, and then the woman, who is definitely not my aunts, laughs again, jogs as fast as she can in the water.

7.

A week passes. In the pool, early, I stand next to this woman who continues to intrigue me, now because she's so different from anyone I thought she was. I ask if the upcoming weekend will be interesting for her. It will be—she's going to a dinner celebrating the Lunar New Year. Then, I ask her name, which I've been guessing at for months. I haven't wanted to know; I have wanted to know. A name makes someone a particular, individual person, immune from my imagination. When she tells me her name, it's beautiful—a flower name, more exotic than any woman in my family can claim. And she tells me her family has been in Los Angeles for generations, so there's no relationship to my center-of-the-country inheritance.

She and I talk about enthusiasms that wane in later life, as well as what we continue to love. We agree to a never-diminishing passion for language. Then I tell her my silly grammar joke: "Past, present and future walked into a bar. It was tense."

That's it. That's the joke. She laughs that big laugh of hers.

8.

She hasn't shown up at the Y now for weeks. I thought there'd be at least another conversation, one that could provide an ending for this meditation on assumptions. Evidently, nothing ends without more questions. I think I have a right to people, to know their motives and reasons, to understand them. I don't.

SPIRIT

"Have you seen the ghost?" Vanessa sits on a box in her living room, where she and her new husband Dylan have lived in the apartment next door to us for three years. They're moving; I've come over to say goodbye. I perch unsteadily on a suitcase in the nearly empty room; Dylan stands in the door to the kitchen.

She goes on, "Dylan didn't believe in ghosts until he actually saw it a few times."

"In the winter, usually," Dylan adds.

Vanessa, an actor, is perpetually upbeat; Dylan, a filmmaker, is restrained, quiet. They're in their mid-twenties, starting out together. Both of them have always been more than willing to befriend my husband and me, older people who could use help carrying groceries or bolting down a new toilet seat.

"Ghosts want to come inside during the cold season," I say. "That's why we give out treats on Halloween to kids dressed in sheets–the treats keep the ghosts outside."

"Wow, I didn't know that," Vanessa says, ready to extend the story. "The ghost is a man. Dark-haired. He appears in the hallway." She turns in the direction of the hall that leads to the bedrooms. I stare into the dim hall, too, as if the ghost might accommodate us and show up if we concentrate hard enough.

"Does he do anything?" "No. He's just there," Dylan says, in a voice even softer than usual.

I mention that although I haven't seen the ghost, every once in a while I glimpse something—a flitting something—between their apartment and ours. This group of seven apartments was built in 1930; our place, in front, is separate from the rest. Dylan and Vanessa's back patio and ours are separated by a walkway that goes toward the laundry room. I sit at our dining room table when I eat breakfast and lunch; I can look out on the walkway. When I sense the whatever-it-is slide past—a black shadow—I try to see if it's a neighbor walking along, or if it's, well, the ghost, I guess, now that Vanessa has named it.

I've always believed in ghosts. These beliefs have deepened into the understanding that two (or more) worlds run parallel to each other, and, at times, the membrane between those worlds thins considerably. That's when spirits make themselves seen, or intuited, or sensed. But, in spite of my brief shadow-sightings, I haven't ever seen a ghost that I could identify in that way. Why was Dylan the one to spot the ghost? Vanessa would have been more receptive. She described Dylan as a non-believer in such things. Perhaps the non-believers are the ones these ghosts visit, to let us know how another world manages without us, that we aren't the only intelligences inhabiting the earth. Since Vanessa and Dylan have moved, I've missed them. Two new tenants, roommates, Patrick and Scott, have taken over the apartment next door. They've been here four months. I barely know them. Shall I ask if they've seen the ghost? For now, I don't.

* * * * * * * * * * *

It's a windy April evening; I sit at our dining room table where I can watch the TV set we have nearby. Baseball season has started; the Dodgers are playing the San Diego Padres. The game is in the first inning.

It's dusk, not dark enough yet for me to pull the drapes closed. The window across from the table rattles in the wind. I glance away from the game for a minute, glad to be safe inside tonight. Low-growing palm fronds flap wildly outside. Then, there's a figure—male, a definite shape: dark head and torso. Surely, this is our neighbor behind his own fence checking on things. He moves quickly. I look in the direction the figure is going, not turning my eyes away, but he disappears even though I'm fully focused on him.

No one is there where someone was present a few seconds ago. Ghost. Our ghost, in the general space he likes to inhabit, near 1254 N. Mariposa, or in that apartment. Just now, did he slip through the wall, go indoors to escape the wind? He seems sure of himself, not a wimpy, opaque bit of protoplasm but a fully masculine spirit who knows where he is.

Why does he come here? Does he need something? Or is he simply visiting, re-living (if that's the word) a time when he rented 1254 or loved somebody who did or perhaps participated in designing and building these Mission-style apartments? Supposedly, this small complex was a showplace in its time. Maybe our ghost is proud to have helped create living space that echoes LA's Spanish/Mexican history, that still offers an artfulness and grace not present in more contemporary, commercially-planned apartments.

But I don't know. I'm not capable of psychic communication with the dead. I can only sympathize. I hope the ghost exists here because he's comfortable, not because he's haunting us—or needs to justify his earthly life by coming back to it, again and again.

I hope he likes us, the melange of tenants which includes Omar, who sings a little too loudly; Angela, his friend in back, upstairs, whose parrot travels on her shoulder; Zack, an artist who put an oversized, blue, papier mache pig on the garage roof; Patrick and Scott; a couple of others we almost never see; Harry and me.

And does the ghost hope we like him? I still haven't asked Patrick and Scott if they've seen him; perhaps he'd be offended if I made too much of his presence. He is, of course, secretive, the ghost in the wind who doesn't pay rent, but who sticks around—silently, persistently included.

TREES

Don was eighty years old, with the look of a handsome man to whom life had been generous, even though it had made him bony and thin—much of that because of the pancreatic cancer he was suffering from, the harsh chemo treatments. He'd had a long run as a comedian; his wife, the red-haired Maybin, was a dancer who'd been in the chorus of Broadway shows and had worked on TV in its early days. The two of them could talk endlessly about themselves, their arts, their youthful careers—never tediously. How did they manage that? I'm no stranger to self-absorption, but I can't pretend to be entertaining about it.

Don was Jewish, from New York; Maybin was a Mississippi girl who'd discovered a glamourous performer within her diminutive body. She fell in love with him when she was working in New York; he asked her for a date, suggested they go to the zoo. No one had ever wanted to take her to the zoo before. Don and Maybin celebrated their fiftieth anniversary with a big party in a suite at the Chateau Marmont in Hollywood, arranged by their daughter, a successful TV producer.

I didn't know Don Sherman as well as my husband Harry did: The two of them videotaped approximately 100 of their conversations about acting, comedy, poetry, life. These went onto the blog they started in 2011, led by David Lloyd Glover, a visual artist who had the technical skill to do the filming and the blog set-up. Don died, inevitably and sadly, when his cancer took over in 2012. He died at home, in the San Fernando Valley house he and Maybin had lived in for years.

One year later at the end of May, Maybin invited fifteen people who cared about Don to come to Forest Lawn Cemetery where a commemorative stone had been placed on his grave. We stood in a circle around the grave to talk about Don, recount anecdotes mostly about his humor. His daughter Amy recalled that once he'd protested: "I'm all alone in my own house—a Jew from New York! My wife is a Christian from the South! My daughter's a Muslim!" This got a laugh. (The last remark was a comment about Amy, who'd once defended the Palestinian position in Israel.) At the end of our stories, Maybin sang, "My Buddy," the old, overly familiar song unexpectedly moving as she, tiny and weepy, called on the stalwart performer in herself to get through the whole thing without faltering.

The group was invited to Maybin and Don's house for lunch. In the spacious back yard, people gathered around a long table to eat and chat. I knew David Glover and his wife Judith; I knew Pearl, a long-time friend of the Shermans; a few others were familiar to me. Ned Rose, Judy's father, 102 or 103 years old, sat across from me. He was visiting from New York. Jack and Margo were at the other end of the table: Jack had been in a number of David Mamet's plays; he and Margo met when he was doing a film in Canada. A woman I didn't know told stories about her childhood, when she and her friends climbed over fences to get to movie lots where they hung out. "Those were our playgrounds," she said.

Pearl, a professional pianist, talked about the movies (many,

many, many) she'd worked on as part of the orchestra that played the movie scores. Ned talked about business—he'd been a successful investor and an important force at the New York Friars' Club. Judy said she'd been asked to direct a new play. (Harry and I had recently seen her Actors' Studio production of "The Dresser.") Amy, the TV producer, and her husband Dan detailed the rise and fall of Amy's show "Bunheads," a series I was sorry to see canceled.

All of this entertainment business talk turned me toward the food, which was Southern, a bow to Maybin's origins, catered and delivered so nobody had to spend hours cooking the rice and beans and gumbo and cornbread, making the overly sweet iced tea. I ate and looked out at the yard, beyond the yard, felt myself let go of the chatter that softened the underlying sorrow we shared because Don wasn't at the table with us. I let go of my need to be especially kind to Maybin, grateful to be included in the day because I wasn't really part of the closely knit group around her. I stopped trying to ask intelligent questions about everybody's memories, to be attentive even when I wasn't really very interested in how Alfred Hitchcock behaved on the set of "The Birds."

There were trees beyond the yard—trees and trees and trees. Their big branches shook in the afternoon breeze that had come up. The leaves glistened and rustled in that way that reminds me of fairy tale forests where witches make magic potions, where talking, helpful animals give advice. The greens of the various trees ranged from vivid shamrock to chartreuse to mossy softness, every color lifted by breeze and sunlight, transformed:

I understood then that the day was about transforming Don's death into this intimate community's mythology, shifting private histories into personal legend. No matter how sophisticated or successful or talented, we're still Nature. But even as we fade toward our endings, we can shimmer a little, like the trees and their beautiful leaves.

A few months before Don died, Harry and I went to a birthday party where there were a lot of strangers. We sat at one table with David and Judy, Don and Maybin, a couple of others. As someone new arrived to sit with us, we had to move our chairs closer together. Don was next to me, shrunken and elfish as he showed me how thin the skin on his hand had gotten from the chemo. When I squeezed my chair closer to Don's to make room, he leaned over to mutter in a conspiratorial tone, "I've waited for this moment," which made me laugh out loud. My sympathy for his cancer ordeal was transformed by his joke into something better than pity or bemoaning our fates. So, a year later, I looked up at the trees beyond his yard, let go of my social self, thought of how everybody once lived in trees, how pleasant that could have been. I thought about going home with Harry to enjoy this spring evening together. "It's all okay," I thought. "It's just fine. It's okay."

LEGS

I. CURB

I've just left Nina, my hair stylist, who's cut my hair as she does every month. My car is parked half a block away, easy enough to get to. But my arthritis and back problems don't allow anything to be easy. I have my cane; I'm doing fine. Then, I come to the curb I have to step down to get to the driver's side of my Nissan. I make a few gestures with my right foot, aiming my foot off the curb. My great fear—typical of all old people—is that I'll fall. Fall and break an ankle, a wrist, sustain a concussion. I've already had back surgery and two hip replacements.

"Well, shit," I'm thinking, ashamed that I can't maneuver a simple curb. A voice behind me says, "Do you need some help?"

A young Asian man with stunningly colorful, well-pressed, salmon-orange jeans is holding out his hand. I take it. That's exactly the gesture I need to make it off the curb. After I say, "Thank you," I tell him, "Those are great pants!" He smiles then rejoins the two people he's been walking with: a woman and child.

This is the year for bright colors. Young style-makers are showing up in chartreuse, electric blue, various shades of orange. They don't often take note of me. I'm not completely surprised that a young, hip, handsome man offers to help me; young people often hold doors open as I hobble into Trader Joe's or the dentist's office. What impresses me is that he isn't shy about so much color.

This is a story about loss, as most stories are—the loss of simple walking, of bright print dresses, confidence in my body. Nina cuts my hair short, short, short. I have nothing to preen about and nothing to hide. My world view has shifted from active participant to witness.

Which is inevitable, isn't it? I climb into my car. Ahead of me, in the yard of the neighborhood pediatrician's office is a "tulip tree," a variety of magnolia that blooms now, in February, here in Southern California. The blossoms are voluptuous, lavender cups. The seasons turn: How vividly the landscape instructs us in this—whatever is lost and can't be regained may, at least, be replaced. Someone helps at the right moment. A dormant tree blooms in February. Beauty is beauty. Rejoice.

2. POLKA

In 1958, I had a boyfriend I really liked. We both went to junior college in Grand Rapids, Michigan, a city where winters are brutal and Calvinism thrives. Dick Grinnewald was only a little taller than I was, which rendered making out in his parents' car easy; there weren't any awkward long legs to get in the way. Dick laughed without ever forcing it. He put his arms around me gently. His light brown hair was soft and clean whenever I smoothed it. And, he wore Old Spice shaving lotion, a wonderfully erotic scent to my inexperienced self.

Dick was Catholic. He'd gone to Catholic High School, alien territory to us Methodists. My father, ever since I could remember, spoke with disdain about Catholics, telling me, "They have to pray to saints. We Protestants go directly to God. There's no middle man for us!"

So, Dad and my step-mother Eleanor were sullen when Dick showed up, but middle class Methodists were less rigid than Calvinists, so they didn't stop us from dating. Dick, to his credit, maintained his good humor, and I was always relieved to get out of my house, into the big Buick that Dick managed to borrow most weekends.

We usually went to the movies. "Gigi," "Vertigo," "The Long Hot Summer," "Cat on a Hot Tin Roof" were all released that year. After a film, we'd eat fried clam rolls at the local Howard Johnson's restaurant, then stop on the way home to kiss and touch—no clothing removed; no actual sex, ever, but there was the thrill and comfort of being loved. I needed that. My mother had died of cancer four years before. I hadn't had time to fully recover before my father married a woman I admired but with whom I had nothing in common. Dick and I had fun together. We cared about each other. That mattered. It mattered more than anything else at the time.

One Saturday night, he was invited to a Polish wedding reception across the river from downtown Grand Rapids. This was where machinists, auto mechanics, short order cooks, waitresses, saleswomen in small clothing shops lived. A couple of Dick's friends from Catholic High had gotten married; he wanted to wish them well, especially since the bride was pregnant. The wedding had been quickly planned to take place before the bride started "to show."

The reception was well under way when we arrived at the Polish community center—one huge room, festooned with colorful paper streamers hung from the ceiling. Tables loaded with food stood on one side of the room; the other three sides were lined with chairs. At the far end was a band. A polka band.

Of course, I could sing, "Roll Out the Barrel"; it was a standard in the 1940s and 50s. But I hadn't seen a live polka band, complete with an accordion player who'd never heard the word "restraint." It was too noisy to talk. I sat down in an unsteady folding chair while Dick went to congratulate the bride and groom then get us some food. Before long, I found myself balancing a flimsy paper plate on my lap, a plate which held hot chunks of Polish sausage, several delicious deep-fried somethings, a slice of white bread. To drink, there was the familiar "red punch" as everybody called it: "Hawaiian Punch," by brand. It came in huge cans; the sugary, fruity contents could be poured into a punch bowl along with ice and a few slices of orange and called a party drink. There were also kegs of beer for anyone who wanted something more substantial.

I wore a dress my step-mother had bought for me when I was graduating from high school and went to a senior class dance, a dress I loved: It was light blue satin covered with white lace. It wasn't a "formal" with gobs of net for a skirt. The dress was simple, stylish, grown up. I had on hose and heels—white linen heels, my high school graduation shoes. Everyone else had dressed up, too, for the wedding, and many people, both women and men, wore gold crosses on slender chains around their throats. This bold show of one's religious beliefs would be unacceptable in my family. Such jewelry was considered tasteless, an undignified showing-off of piety. (We smugly kept our piety to ourselves.)

Dancers zipped past. The music never stopped. Dick and I liked to dance together; our similar heights made us a good pair. The polka is basically stomp, stomp, bounce, so I didn't have any trouble picking up the steps. My legs were strong. They kept moving, moving, stomping, bouncing. A large, older man with rings of sweat under the arms of his white shirt cut in. Dick stepped aside. The man swept me into a wild, super-fast polka. We danced until I couldn't breathe.

When I got home, the linen shoes were ruined, scuffed beyond hope. Linen can't be polished. I had runs in my hose. The dress was okay, although I can't remember wearing it again after that night. I'd been "on the other side of the river" where people weren't afraid of accordions or sweaty underarms or spicy sausage. My family couldn't imagine I wanted a different life from theirs, and I had no way of articulating that yet. Soon, Dick would drop out of school, head for an acting career in New York. He didn't break my heart, but he certainly cracked it in several vulnerable places.

I'd go on to finish college, then be plunged into early adulthood where I would make the terrible mistakes necessary for me to finally understand what I needed. But in my first glimpse of an Otherness I might aspire to, the Catholics helped. I learned, from Dick, to say, "Hail Mary, full of grace..." and so on. I prayed that prayer every night in Grand Rapids, whispering to Mary, a compassionate mother, "Pray for us now..."

3. INFANT

My mother has put me in my playpen, along with toys to keep me occupied while she works in the kitchen, a few feet from our living room, where I am. The playpen is an acreage to me, large enough that every corner is a new territory. I crawl easily, picking up my Sunny Sue rag doll, then dropping her when the red and blue tin top catches my attention. I haven't learned to spin the top yet, but I can shove it back and forth, hoping it will somehow start to whirl on its own. I'm an only child, so I can learn what I need by myself, which usually suits me.

The playpen is enclosed by rounded wooden posts, set four or five inches apart. Looking out, I see the open kitchen door, hear my mother singing a little while she cooks. As I crawl to the side of the playpen, it occurs to me that I can reach out for the posts and hold onto them, one in each hand. As I try this, a thrilling sensation starts in my legs: The feeling makes me want to pull myself up on my feet. After a few tries, I stand up as I clutch the posts.

My mother walks in to check on me. When she sees me standing, just before I plunk myself down on my butt again, she smiles and claps her hands, obviously pleased. More than pleased, because she keeps up the smiles and encouragement, which I don't understand because I haven't done anything except follow the impulses in my legs. I see my mother walk to the big black telephone nearby. After she dials—the phone clicks with every number—I can tell by the sound of her voice that she's talking to my father; I recognize the rhythm of his name and then my own. I've stood on my feet! That's the miracle she's telling him about.

I'll be able to walk soon. And that eventually will lead to roller skating, bike riding, playing on the trapeze my dad will make for me in our back yard. I'll want to be in the circus, although my mother says, "Oh, honey, I don't think you'd like that kind of life."

Eventually, I'll get off the trapeze, leave elementary school, walk through the halls of Northeast Junior High, where I'll fall in desperate love with Eddie Loomis, more broad-shouldered and lower-voiced than the other seventh grade boys. He has wonderful corduroy shirts: one, a deep forest green; another, burgundy red. I quickly find out that Eddie adores my friend Sondra Whalen, so I keep my desperation to myself, walk past Eddie simply saying, "Hi," never even trying to start a conversation. He and Sondra are a couple from that first autumn onward. It doesn't occur to me to seduce Eddie away from her. I have no seductive moves in me. My body is barely able to adjust to the onslaught of hormones it has to handle, much less figure out what Jerry Lee Lewis means: "... a wiggle in her walk, a giggle in her talk make the world go round..."

The world would keep turning, keep "going round" without my feminine wiles. I'd keep walking. Life outside the sweetness of my family's encouragement –"She's on her feet!

Holly pulled herself up! Our baby's on her feet"– wasn't a miracle. It wasn't the circus. It became the task of keeping my own secrets—oh, Eddie! As that independent only child, this seemed natural, if lonely. In the future, I would get lonelier; I'd also treasure my private inner life, the beginning of individuality and personal choice.

The tin top was a consistent part of my infancy, and I did, soon, discover how to press down the plunger sticking out so that the top spun and spun. We come into the world to figure out who we are, what we can do. I could decode a mysterious toy. I could walk and keep walking.

4. T'AI CHI

We gathered in a dance practice room at LA City College, a not-too-spacious void, one wall completely mirrored. Eight or nine of us in "comfortable clothes and flat shoes," as instructed in the catalogue, waited for the t'ai chi teacher, who, when he arrived, was old, small, expressionless. A baseball cap covered what we'd discover to be his completely bald head. He set down a grocery bag that I knew from last semester's class held copies of a sheet with drawings of t'ai chi moves, supposedly helpful but really only pictures of a pudgy guy swinging his arms.

This was my second attempt at the beginners' t'ai chi class, taught by Marvin Smalheiser, who, if expressionless, was aware of each of us and understood what we needed from him. It wasn't the Xerox copies; it was Marvin himself, demonstrating the simple lifting and lowering of arms which begins the first section of the Yang Style Long Form he taught. Then, on to Grasp Bird Tail Right and Grasp Bird Tail Left.

I was sixty-five years old, finally learning this exercise/art I'd wanted to have as my own for thirty years, since a visit to a t'ai chi class in Bronson Park where a pontificating Chinese man talked for a long time in an accent which made understanding him impossible to me. We –twenty or so hopefuls–eventually lined up on the grass and stood there. More talk. I don't recall that we moved any part of our bodies, although I assumed this line of people would lead to some sort of t'ai chi move. When the class was over, I headed home, puzzled. Was I incredibly stupid, not getting anything the man said or understanding the purpose of the standing in line? Probably. I never went back.

In the intervening years, I read the LACC extension catalogue every time it showed up in the mail, read the description of the beginning t'ai chi class and wanted to join. Timing is everything, as the general wisdom goes, so when I'd written enough all that time to see a book of my "selected poems and prose" published, I realized that even though I had more to write, this was a good moment to plunge into t'ai chi. I had enough space in my life, in my mind, in my body for something other than writing.

I had no physical memory, as dancers do. I had no experience with Chinese martial arts. During the first beginners' class, I'd stumbled through the lessons, practiced diligently at home and still been woefully inept. By now, though, I knew Marvin a little and a couple of people from his Saturday morning classes in Griffith Park, classes free to anybody who wanted to continue with t'ai chi, learn all three of the sections of The Form, take on the history, the complications of this beautiful art.

The park: I know Griffith Park well, but I couldn't find the t'ai chi class on my first three Saturday tries; as I drove home, frustrated, I realized I was being tested. Did I sincerely want to keep at this art I was so ignorant about? Did I want to opt for humility, for being the old lady who took longer than anyone else to learn every movement? No. Yes. Okay. No. But I kept driving every Saturday, finally spotting one of the women I recognized from the LACC class. She waved at me when I slowed down to ask directions.

"Right over there!" she said, pointing to a shady spot surrounded by trees, circled by gentle hills.

"Right over there" was where I spent the next year and a half learning The Form. The whole Form. When I despaired, Marvin told me that Confucius had written, "Some learn after one or two tries. Others need many tries. Everyone ends up in the same place, knowing the same thing." This was reassurance I still recite to myself—about much more than t'ai chi.

Doing The Form every week with a dozen or so practiced t'ai chi devotees gave me a rare sense of the universal physical and psychic energy under us all. We weren't perfect, but we were synchronized. We weren't in total balance, but we were earnestly working on, as Marvin said, "Our contradictions." T'ai chi is an art of yang/yin, of bringing one's inner arguments into conversation with each other. When I once asked Dan, a man who'd been doing t'ai chi for a long time, a lost soul but not without grace, why he started to do t'ai chi, he said, "Once, I saw some people doing it. It looked as if they were in another dimension. I wanted to be there, too."

So did I. My feet managed to turn themselves in and out; my very American legs carried me through Chinese poses with names like Snake Creeps Down and Parting the Wild Horse's Mane. I loved those names. Finally, I came to love my willingness to be the oldest, the least proficient, the least flowing and most struggling one of the bunch. No one criticized me except my own ridiculous inner pride. After seven years, I couldn't do any more. My back, always a problem, defeated me.

I've failed at t'ai chi, which I believed I'd practice until the end of my life. Over time, I've found that my strongest beliefs have nothing to do with my fate. For a few years, though, I began to understand how to use my body—arms, legs, waist, spine—in a way that carried me, once in awhile, to another dimension, a good place where contradictions fade, where I became both yang and yin, creative and receptive, noble and absurd.

5. CAT

Many evenings now, I sit, put my legs up on the chair opposite me next to the round oak table where my husband and I have eaten dinner. Our obese, elderly cat Egypt jumps into the chair, settles at my feet. I use one stockinged foot to pet her smooth, gray back; tuck the other foot under her plump body where she keeps it warm.

From this comfortable spot, I watch TV: Maybe a show on the Food Network where a celebrity chef swiftly prepares a dish with trendy ingredients I'll never, ever have in my kitchen—stinging nettles or exotic seaweed or reindeer steaks on a bed of birch twigs. If it's Thursday night, I look at "The Vampire Diaries," one series I've watched from the beginning three or four years ago. It's not the handsome vampire brothers or the heroine's turmoil over which brother she loves. It's not the proliferation of super-natural creatures—wow, here come the "hybrids," who are both werewolf and vampire! It's really my fascination with a plot that grows more and more intricately tangled. My legs up, cat snuggled into my feet, I wait for the moment when the Salvatore brothers and Elena Gilbert and every human, vampire, witch and werewolf in Mystic Falls will explode in an act of spontaneous combustion from the pile upon pile of plot devices and characters' motives that are finally insupportable even on the fantastical planet we know as television.

This is the pleasure of old legs: watching others create upheaval for themselves, having had enough of that myself in past years. I don't roast reindeer; Harry and I eat turkey breast or halibut. He makes the best cheeseburgers I've ever tasted. In spite of physical diminishment, I can cook in our tiny kitchen, reaching easily from sink to counter to oven. Our two cats, Rose along with Egypt, sniff around my feet for treats. I try to resist their begging; Harry doesn't, which isn't good for their weight, but they're old, too, and how much should we deny them? Deny ourselves? Home is our story to create, our planet to inhabit. No vampires. Just us and a couple of extra bags of Science Diet Hairball Control cat food—we never want to run out of that.

LOVE

Tonight, my husband Harry and I are eating Stouffer's vegetable lasagne, frozen dinners I've heated in the oven. There's kale salad from our neighborhood Von's supermarket, plus whole wheat rolls. Not my finest culinary attempt, but okay for Thursday night as we watch an American League baseball playoff game between Detroit and Boston. We're hoping our Dodgers will be in the World Series; they just might be playing either of these AL teams.

"I like watching you eat your vegetable lasagne," Harry says tenderly, as a Detroit outfielder makes a spectacular catch.

Harry's comment is unexpected, so sincere that I'm touched. Ever since we fell in love in 1977, Harry has been a surprise. In the first dream I ever had about him, he jumped at me from behind a door. At 6' 1", Harry's nearly a foot taller than I am, and stronger. He didn't mean to scare me; he wanted to hug me. But I was shaken. Everything about love is about being shaken— my plans suddenly changed; my daily list of tasks rendered useless.

Yesterday, Harry suffered from one of those awful "twenty-four hour flus," as we call them: He vomited in the early morning then collapsed into bed where he slept all day. Toward evening, he woke up long enough to eat a cheese sandwich but fell asleep again until this morning. Now, he's fine. I worried, of course, even recognizing the symptoms, having been through them myself. What if he stayed sick? What if it got worse and worse? I want to save Harry from every terrible possibility. My fierce desire to protect him comes from forces beyond my personal power—the ancient Greeks named these goddesses and gods, Eros being the god of love whose arrows pierce the vulnerable heart and can't be dislodged.

* * * * * * * * * *

This morning, the morning after the lasagne, I lie in bed, waking up, listening to a bird outside. It's October, not mating season. In spring, the mockingbirds are unceasingly musical, but they've been quiet all summer. I listen to the bird's song: It is a song, not just dissonant vocalizing. I remember a dream I've had recently about a star making its way from the sky to land in front of me on the ground, asking for my attention but certainly not belonging to me. These beautiful astonishments. What do we do with them? A wise person I know says, "You stand there in wonder and awe."

Harry sleeps next to me as the bird embellishes its aria. I usually wake up in the morning feeling as if I should hurry to get things done. But this morning, the bird and the memory of my falling star dream and Harry snoozing calmly—healthy, now: I get out of bed to feed the cats knowing the day will be taken care of, no matter how much or how little I do.

* * * * * * * * * *

The moon is huge and full and self-confident. It's outside this window, high in the early morning sky. The moon controls ocean tides; the moon controls love. Lunar logic isn't logic but magic. Magic controls love.

Love's enchantment is a spell I've been under in the years Harry and I have been together. I believe we're all possessed by angels and by the tragedies we call demons. Love is divine healing, along with the awakening of fears, angers, madnesses we'd get rid of if we could, if we weren't human, if we weren't, inescapably, grand tangles of sweet lettuces and poisonous roots.

Under a spell: Because of my mother's much too early death, I fear abandonment. It took me a long time to recognize Harry's solid loyalty. He'd tell me, "I'm here," when we first knew each other, but I wasn't sure. Even now, even when I am sure, if he's gone what I feel is too long, if he's out in the city doing errands, seeing friends, just living his active life, I worry. I would never ask him to stay right next to me every minute—I wouldn't even like that—but the spell that's been cast over me includes the dictum that loss is the result of love: Those you love the most will be lost the soonest.

The moon's phases are startling: from new to sliver to crescent to half to full and then waning, but they're predictable; the moon assures me that whatever moves life ecstatically or sorrowfully, eventually there will be safety once more. The moon will be full. The moon will be gone. The moon will be full.

* * * * * * * * * * *

Now I'm the one who's sick, not very sick, but sick enough to feel nauseous and exhausted, to fall asleep especially early on Tuesday night. It's autumn. It's the time when chilly mornings and nights remind me that the world is hunkering down, quieting, turning away from light and good humor. A bird makes a crackling sound: fire catching hold in dry grass.

So, I feel crappy and frightened, not for any big reason, not because I'm having a heart attack or a stroke or anything life-threatening, but just because my body can't get comfortable with itself. The next morning, Wednesday, I'm better but solemn. As I'm slowly washing a few breakfast dishes, Harry calls out to me, "I'm going to Skylight to pick up that book I ordered. Do you want me to get something for dinner?" I say, "Yes!" He says, "Do you want me to surprise you?" I say, "Yes!" This is a very different surprise from the shock of my first dream of Harry, leaping from behind a door, unintentionally scaring me. This is about both of us knowing what we like to eat. This will be food to share as the first game of the World Series gets under way tonight. (No, the Dodgers didn't make it this year.) This is home, antidote to fear.

* * * * * * * * * *

Some weeks later, a Sunday: Harry reads to me from the *LA Times* about a new Frederick Wiseman documentary, its subject matter U.C. Berkeley. The film is four hours long, culled from 250 hours of film. Imagine: four hours from 250. The crystallization of our human sprawl and mess. Simplification—the naturally efficient: our slender wrist bones, our capable inner ear. The husband who manages a compliment about his wife's eating lasagne.

The fulfillment of love is its paring down, that original arrow aimed at the heart now firmly embedded, still sometimes piercing but more often an integral part of the body—ingrown, familiar, moving right along with my hands.

When Harry walks through our hallway, sees me in the study writing, he often calls out, "There's Holly!" assuring me that I am where I am, doing what I'm doing. Love affirms reality. Love is, more and more as I age and struggle with my body, the body itself: the woman I was; the woman I've become.

I reassure him, as well. I do this for the pleasure of seeing him turn his head to one side as he's done since I met him, shy and happy when I say, too, "There's Harry!"

AUTHOR'S BIO

Holly Prado has had eleven books published, including poetry, prose-poetry, a novel and two novellas. Her poetry and prose have appeared in numerous publications, including *The Paris Review*, *The Kenyon Review*, *The American Poetry Review* and many others. The winter 2012-2013 issue of *Malpaís Review* published her fifteen page poem/letter to TuFu, the Tang Dynasty poet. In 2015, poems were included in *Wide Awake: Poets of Los Angeles and Beyond*, an anthology of over 100 poets (Pacific Coast Poetry Series). Poems also appeared in the 2015 anthology *Edgar Allan Poet #3 --2015* (Edgar and Lenore's Publishing House).

Since the early 1970s, Prado has taught creative writing both privately and in alternative educational situations, such as the Los Angeles Woman's Building and Beyond Baroque Literary Foundation. From 1989-2009, she taught poetry in the Master of Professional Writing Program at USC.

In 2000, she was awarded First Prize in the Fin de Millennium competition, sponsored by the Los Angeles Poetry Festival.

In November, 2006, she was presented with a Certificate of Recognition from the City of Los Angeles for her achievements in writing, teaching and participation in the Los Angeles literary community. She is the 2016 recipient of the George Drury Smith Award for Outstanding Achievement in Poetry, given annually by Beyond Baroque Literary Foundation, founded in 1968 by George Drury Smith.

Prado lives in East Hollywood with her husband Harry Northup, a film actor and poet. They are both founding members of Cahuenga Press, a poets publishing cooperative which has been publishing books of poetry since 1989.

Really Truly was written in 2013.